EPHEMERON

Southern Messenger Poets

Dave Smith, Series Editor

EPHEMERON

POEMS

T. R. HUMMER

Louisiana State University)|(Baton Rouge

Published by Louisiana State University Press
Copyright © 2011 by T. R. Hummer
All rights reserved
Manufactured in the United States of America
LSU Press Paperback Original
First printing

Designer: Michelle A. Neustrom
Typefaces: Whitman, text; Penumbra MM, display
Printer and binder: IBT Global

Library of Congress Cataloging-in-Publication Data

Hummer, T. R.
    Ephemeron : poems / T.R. Hummer.
        p. cm. — (Southern messenger poets)
    "LSU Press Paperback original"—T.p. verso.
    Includes bibliographical references.
    ISBN 978-0-8071-3987-5 (pbk. : alk. paper) — ISBN 978-0-8071-3988-2
(pdf) — ISBN 978-0-8071-3989-9 (epub) — ISBN 978-0-8071-3990-5 (mobi)
    I. Title.
    PS3558.U445E64 2012
    811'.54—dc22

                                                          2011011946

Some poems in this collection have previously appeared in various publications, print and online, and the author
makes grateful acknowledgment, as follows:

AntiPoetry: "Toxins" and "Implosions"; *Ascent:* "Case History"; *Connotation Press:* "Interrogations," "Abandon," and
"Ad Hominem"; *Cutthroat:* "Ephemer," "Ephemera," "Biography of Eros," "Inventory," and "Notes for an Epitaph";
Gulf Coast: "Landscape with the Scent of Scorching Cabbage," "Minor Epic with a Misread First Line from Yannis
Ritsos," and "Melancholia for Dummies"; *Kenyon Review:* "Ephemeron"; *Lake Effect:* "Rather than Nothing";
Linebreak: "Argument from Design"; *Mayday:* "Memoir," "From Abroad," and "Assimilation"; *Mudlark:* "System,
Fallacy of Composition," "Bald Man Fallacy," "Infinite by Virtue of Its Everlastingness," "Bounded by Its Own
Completeness," and "The Illegibility of Providence"; *New South:* "Canon," "Theory," and "Fallacy"; *Ninth Letter:*
"Either," "/," and "Or"; *Northwest Review:* "A Catalog of Landscapes Viewed in a Claude Glass" and "Registry of the
Corpses, the Arrangement of which is a Reverse Chronology According to Death Date"; *Normal School:* "Nothing
Beautiful Except that which Does Not Exist," "Everything in the Past is a Particle," and "Everything in the Future
is a Wave"; *The Rumpus:* "Work Order and Schematic"; *Slate:* "Bad Infinity" and "The Unwritten History of Prose";
Two Weeks: "Erotic Manual"; *Valparaiso Review:* "Everything that Is the Case" and "Evening Report."

The paper in this book meets the guidelines for permanence and durability of the Committee on Production
Guidelines for Book Longevity of the Council on Library Resources. ∞

For Theo and Jackson

I was in a Printing house in Hell & saw the method in which knowledge is transmitted from generation to generation.

—WILLIAM BLAKE

He seeks one who has vanished, who in turn sought one who had vanished, and so on.

—MICHEL DE CERTEAU

CONTENTS

III. EPHEMERA

EPHEMERON

I

EPHEMERON

EPHEMERON

Those are windflowers glowing in the outer darkness
    just beyond the gateposts. If I squint,
I see them clearly: white windflowers, flicker of star gas,
    bridal-veil nebula—an infinity bent
By the gravity of dawn and rain, but opening.
    It astonishes me again: I am fifty and pregnant,
And beyond the bedroom window September is gathering
    its cosmological light. *A child,* the windflower says.
What's that? Nothing. Or hardly anything
    five weeks beyond conceiving. And that monstrous
Morning star above the neighbor's gable mutters,
    enough. What's one more human? Heartless,
These elemental things, mist on the sidewalk, litter:
    And so there are gods again, suddenly.
The windflower opens its oblivious scripture
    as the sun advances degree by omniscient degree.
In the street a shadow of sparrows echoes the oil slick
    left by yesterday's downtown express. Details gather ominously,
And that is the point, precisely, a god's favorite trick—
    the accrual, like money in the bank, of our undoing.
But an arm's length away, the anti-entropic
    womb of my sleeping wife is growing
A consciousness. Listen, zygote. The windflower's true name:
    Anemone. Its true vocation: to be blowing
Against a wooden gate at 6 a.m.
    in the broken dawn-light of the fiftieth September
Of a man old enough to refuse to be ashamed
    of his own joy. And the windflower's fate? No matter.
It is enough, now, to watch it being.
    It is enough to be myself—again almost a father,
Watching the newsboy wander the street—feeling,
    almost, the old gods' abstract hearts contract.
I smell them gather above me like ravens, wheeling
    over the promise my body makes. Black-

Hearted godhood has left them hungry.
   But it is they who assemble, in the amniotic sac,
Bits of star-grit, skeins of DNA, the holy chemistry
   of existence. What can I do but leave them to it, even
Knowing what I know? My spiritual autobiography
   is a shambles-in-progress, my unfinished *Confessions*
A creaking stylized fiction from a distant century—
   it reads like a pirated version of a bad translation
Of a novel the young Balzac wrote, then threw away.
   No god forgives such things. The gods have taste.
Smelling an uncouth sulfur in the aura of the coming day,
   the Supreme Will wrinkles the Great Face.
The Gaze averts, and here's our chance. A space
   opens—ambiguous territory, zygote. Translucent. Our place.

INTERROGATIONS

At dinner, he sat silent, staring at his plate while the others chatted—a ringing in his ears, a gray aura around the chop, sulfurous mist.

The astronomer closed his dome at dawn. The morning star incised the horizon with a smell of lilies and a circle of blood on the eyepiece.

The old woman in the wheelchair watched raindrops inscribe the window. She read its poem to her blind friend, who mumbled protest: too fast.

She pauses on the bridge and looks down. Something about the way water moves, about light. But the child pulls her skirt, crying *time, time.*

They sat on the bridge rail drinking wine in starlight, watching for meteors to etch their glass-cutter lineage into what passed for future.

Dying, by then, seemed normal to her, a breath and another breath and nothing, a stone dropped in water continuing in water to be a stone.

In pinewoods at midnight the trapped weasel, gnawing its own leg, stops to consider its bitter self-taste.

Horses in a meadow over strata of loess and limestone, reflections limned through the meniscus of earth by fossilized skeletons of dolphins.

That singular point on the continuum from which time reads like an inscribed transparency: just ahead, the hospital bed, the miraculous IV.

SYSTEM

When they cut the geneticist open, their blades revealed
    a schematic of precise and interlocking logic
So familiar that the men with bayonets stepped back—
    not in wonder but in the numbness that comes
From infinite repetition. So much complexity
    the genome wrote. Such a simple answer.

TOXINS

Day-old snow under a stone sky at midnight: and beyond flattened trees, in the shadow of a rust-eaten combine, one animal invisibly moving.

❧

The man with the rifle in the blind sits still; his uniform chafes but he cannot move or the face in his scope might ghost and go on living.

❧

Wind-driven dust eats at this rock face as it has for centuries, leaving its tracery of scars, its crows-feet, the aneurysm of erosion.

❧

The blind girl in the library passes her hands over dusty spines like a pianist, like a pickpocket.

❧

The translucence of agate. Shade of the blue fir. Track of a slug, luminous in starlight. Garbage truck. Brickbat. A dead mouse in the wall.

❧

If you hadn't recalled the cabbage and turned suddenly back, the man in the suit would never have lost his pistol. Osmosis. Wages of gnosis.

❧

A dark chamber in the spine of the boar holds the ozone-colored powder that crystallizes his hunger. He lives in his body only. Die for him.

❧

Her eyes convulsed, then closed as the soldier entered her, grinding against her belly the rifle's muzzle, the bracket securing the bayonet.

✥

Dawn should be immaculate, burning you clean, but smoke pours out of the wreckage, shrapnel, and a photograph of you on the train, waving.

LANDSCAPE WITH THE SCENT
OF SCORCHING CABBAGE

A vacuous prairie, dark except for one
    tiny adobe house in scandalous disrepair.
I lived there three or four incarnations ago,
    half-naked and farting, innocent of table manners.
Impossible now to understand how familiar it was.
    It reflected me like a lover, fitted me
Like the fine tailored suit I could never have imagined.
    I was the pig in the baking sty, I was the glorious outhouse.
And the crazed crock on the stove: out of that,
    what miracle will my self serve my soul this time?

MINOR EPIC WITH A MISREAD FIRST LINE
FROM YANNIS RITSOS

They left me dead down in the plain
    where ironweed flailed a turnip field.
After the onslaught, this silence: inexplicable,
    deeper than the crater, where a couple of grunts
Played statue. And beyond the smoking differential
    of a ruptured manure truck, an ambulance driver
Walked, dangling his keys, dragging a siphon.

ABANDON

Silence in the house, people gone out, cats sleeping, leaf blowers put away, the half life of the crawl space ticking down toward zero.

☙

A wind in the desolation of the closet, incremental movement like the shifting of tectonic plates, while in the wall a mouse skull settles.

☙

In a bathroom drawer there are artifacts: molecules of talcum, dried smear of cat's blood, a lingering odor of unidentifiable ointment.

☙

After the journey, months of wandering through landscapes of bone and salt, we came at last to a prairie, a rotting expanse of Persian carpet.

☙

The cleaning finally ended. If there were beds, they would never be made; dishes would stay stained in eternity, and gravity be abolished.

☙

A crack at the center, where even the intelligence of cockroaches was tested: rain eroded the foundation and a simple domesticity entered.

☙

That characteristic turbulence, elemental disturbance in the aether, the tureen vibrating on the sideboard invisibly in the vacant hallway.

☙

Soon, but not yet, the incremental creaking of hinges, the end of molecular bonding, release of form: shapelessness in the doorframe, soon.

AD HOMINEM

A pedestal table by the window, littered with paper—
    fliers, bills, clipped coupons. A basket
Of laundry on the floor, clothes clean for the folding.
    An empty bowl that should hold water for a cat.
Now that people have vanished, who will deal
    with the swarm of tiny annoyances that defined
Human existence? Who will be bothered? What god will try
    to train the cat to shake its head and curse?

ARGUMENT FROM DESIGN

The failing kidney is a portal—the leaky
    heart valve, the clot, the lesion in the brain:
All doors unlocking themselves. Likewise
    outside the body: the razorblade,
The bottle of barbiturates, the utility pole
    beside the curve in the icy highway,
The rifle over the mantelpiece (it *must*
    go off). He understands the radio
On the shelf by the bath in particular
    as a crystal hatchway, hermetically unsealing,
Leading, after a prelude of unspectacular
    fireworks, to a region beyond
The invention of the hinge and the hasp,
    where jamb and lintel are less
Than ugly rumors, and nobody has
    a key to worry over, wear out,
Misplace, twist off, or jangle obsessively.

FALLACY OF COMPOSITION

The noon sky darkens with flying bodies: the extinct birds
    live in the mind, therefore the extinct birds live.
The color of the day deepens with memory. All the wreckage
    of history is eclipsed. The blacksmith raises his hammer,
And the red hot horseshoe straightens into an iron bar.
    Consciousness moves like a shadow in the forest
And whole peoples are restored. An arrow flies
    over a rabbit's shoulder and the rabbit continues,
But the children eat nevertheless. The body testifies
    without speaking: by walking upright
It makes visible what lies within. Another artillery shell
    is canceled, another family prays and falls asleep.
A place remains at the empty table for the son
    who was vaporized. A bed is made and waits
Though the others sleep on the floor. In the silent house
    nobody hears the couple who struggle to conceive
How the mind will bring him back, how the fact is broken.

BAD INFINITY

During the colonoscopy, orbiting through twilight sleep,
    she felt, light-years distant in the interior darkness, a thump
And a dull but definite pain—as if someone were dragging,
    at the end of a rusty chain, a transistor radio through her body,
A small beige box with a gold grill, assembled by a child in southeast Asia
    in 1964—and she woke in groggy panic till the nurse made soothing noises
For her to sleep by, like a song in an alien language heard through static
    beamed from the far side of Arcturus: The Dave Clark Five's
"Glad All Over," maybe, tuned in by a boy in Thailand. *Such a drug,*
    the doctor said. *Everything you feel you will forget.*
Amen to that. Amen to plastic and silicon, amen to a living wage,
    amen to our tinny music, to the shrapnel in the IV drip,
Amen to the template of genes that keeps the body twitching,
    and the wormhole in the gut of Orion I will slip through
When the chain breaks and the corroded battery bursts, its acids eating
    all the delicate circuitry that binds the speaker to the song.

ASSIMILATION

Even his fingerprints vanished. His skin smoothed like river stone; his grip
on the world diminished. He was sliding someplace frictionless.

Lovers had become landscape—the woman he knew that ancient summer
was lost in a hedgerow, flowering, leaving, framing what could be seen.

What he touched penetrated skin and clung, but he did not want to release
the pen, sofa, wallet: they defined him as the boundaries faded.

The walls of the house have thickened, the rooms grown smaller; the foyer
is just the size of a mailbox, and he gropes there for his bills.

Part of him was lost, two fingers from the right hand. His music suffered.
When he played the piano, there was a shadow in the treble, a deadness.

Human emotion reduced him; every passion wore off a layer of skin, every
rage took a subsection of organ. Eroded, he walked through walls.

He now remembers the path forgotten all his life: it leads to a ruined door
through which everything vanishes, even the key that opens it.

FALLACY OF ACCIDENT

Phallus, fallacy, and *fool* sound vaguely alike,
    so all must be related in a deep etymology,
Like the ellipse of shadow on the adobe wall
    is related to the copper birdbath casting it,
And also to the wall, and so to the street beyond,
    and to the market across the street, where bins
Of oranges and lettuces are related to the herd
    of schoolboys staring at the flipped motorbike
In the gutter, and the helmetless body of the man,
    and the litter of morning papers scattered
From his panniers—news of the world, the actor's wedding,
    restaurant reviews, cartoons with banana peels,
Forgetfulness, slippage, gravity, falling bodies.

BIOGRAPHY OF EROS

The witnessing of things in the mind. But what mind? The lovers lay on the bed, handcuffed, saying *Please,* and just for a moment one of them knew.

Sleeping, one of them moaned. It was the dream of the interpenetration of souls. Death is in everything, crystalline arsenic dissolved in alcohol.

They wore raptor masks. One used a small flexible whip. Its marks were radiant traces of ichor. Thus the walls of the sanctum were broken.

They knew it was insanity, and accepted it, but differently. One thought: madness, endlessly. The other thought: madness, finally.

In the dream words were absence. An empty book had contained all truth but for one false letter. He, or was it she, read the other's shadow.

Inside the penumbra there was no dying—death, yes, always, but no motion except the back and forth of the body, the thrust, and the scream.

Entropy, etiolation, emptiness: nothing left but the bed, and the lovers on the bed, and the galaxy surrounding them, dark matter ascendant.

RATHER THAN NOTHING

Stark, luminous, thick-laced morning clouds
    appear and clarify over a blank valley
As if there were nothing in the universe but matter,
    even light condensed to a material thing
You might mine from the sky's impacted veins.
    Weighty thought. To move it, you need sweat
And a pickax, a helmet with a carbide lamp,
    leverage. Images have mass
Like dust in a convoluted shaft where the only sound
    is the miner's grunt and the faint note the notorious
Canary releases, strangling in airlessness.

BALD MAN FALLACY

The sniper's scope passes over the forehead of a girl
    playing with a block of wood in a drainage ditch,
Moves across the neck of her brother—who teases her
    by throwing dried goat turds like meringue bombs
To destroy her battleship—and comes to rest on the heart
    of their mother, who sits in the shade of a date palm,
Carding wool. *Her hands,* he thinks without focusing there,
    are quick and accurate. Raising his viewfinder
With his quick and accurate hands, he sees her lips
    are moving: She sings as she works, a quiet song likely,
But from here he is deaf to her. Probably her song is ancient,
    and if he knew the culture, if he knew her language,
He could read her lips through his gun sight.
    He's in no hurry. It's hot in the niche where he hides—
Sweat runs down from his helmet and pools
    on his ammo box—but he is not disturbed.
His weapon contains a great wind from the wilderness.
    If you shoot them one by one, you will never kill them all.

IMPLOSIONS

Smell of iron in the wind off the mesa—the man at the desk looks up, tasting axhead, knife blade, ghost's chains, his mother's womb blood.

Before bed, turning out the last light in the house, she saw the chemical formula for darkness inscribe itself inside her eyelids.

He felt ill and laid down as the last bus disappeared into the tunnel with men in suits reading headlines, the markets sliding into fever.

In the poem, a girl in a library sleeps, her face on a book; I read her skin in its paper, spot of drool in the margin, a hair in the gutter.

All the angels in Rilke gather at the bookshop to argue with Whitman: who touches this book touches what?

A couple in a convertible at midnight, arguing bitterly; moon half eroded by the solar wind; at roadside a dead coyote, half eaten by ants.

Willows laced over the pond water of history, their image fractured by the ordnance of a war only the dead remember, or a simple wind.

What happened at the end, when everyone thought there was no one left to think, was simple: they forgot it all had ended, and went on.

There was always filth, someone had to touch it, love it, lest it fade like the traces, eons after, at great distance, of a burnt-out star.

At the end of the world an empty beach, empty sea, empty wind, flat, lifeless, leaving nothing behind but its poisonous etching of salt.

NOTHING BEAUTIFUL EXCEPT THAT
WHICH DOES NOT EXIST

A wracked-up Pontiac idles in the rain, its mindless stereo wasting
　　half a city block with a bass line that could liquefy brick.
No one seems to notice. Life, as we say, goes on—*life* defined
　　as the space that opens between concealment and concealment.
Shop windows rattle. A cashier nurses his migraine. This is not
　　the apocalypse of music, but the technology of a volume
That can never be filled. Reckon the area of a vacuum. Compute
　　the circumference of the economy of Lebanon.
The car goes on broadcasting its formal lesson: form dissolves.
　　It has the incalculable half-life of a dirty bomb.

EVERYTHING IN THE PAST IS A PARTICLE

Having discovered the true name
    of the infinite, she utters it and vanishes,
Whereupon she finds herself in a vaguely familiar
    hallway lined with numbered doors,
And, opening the one marked 3, she enters a garden,
    a birthday party, where a small child crushed
With disappointment is crying with that passion
    adults can scarcely imagine giving
In to—and *Yes*, she thinks, *this is holiness*,
    and she bows and reassumes
Her unassuageable selfhood, to dwell in it
    forever, the promise broken, the gift
Refused, three candles flickering but never going out.

EVERYTHING IN THE FUTURE IS A WAVE

That hurtling into nothing, that familiar, sickening
    thrownness, that falling-down-the-elevator-shaft
Vacuity in the belly—the image of the crushed child etched
    on a retina and walking through the walls
Of the skull: or simply my death contained
    in the shadow of a hawk launched on a stiff wind,
The distraction of that black motion, the car that skids,
    the retaining wall, the fountaining of blood
As the blown bird flies, oblivious of the wreckage
    or even of the unconscious shadow that rushes on to nowhere.

MELANCHOLIA FOR DUMMIES

The sun has exploded in a black sky, but the angel,
    preoccupied by demons of his own devising, stares fixedly
Into a middle distance only angels care about. Dürer
    was onto something, but meditation is overrated.
While the angel was tilting at mantras, his dog was fading,
    dear faithful Cosmo, he who had followed
Through all the rings of Being and the ten thousand zones
    of torment, he who never questioned
The wisdom of flying, or cursing god, or dancing
    on the heads of pins—old unquestioning creature
Not nagging or asking why or where as he was dragged
    by a leash of molten gold from torture to beatitude,
Garden to comet, sin to blessing to vastation—worn out
    with his master's infinite dissatisfied agitation,
He closed his eyes. And you, winged genius of despair,
    you want to know why you are thus blighted with angst?
God takes his vengeance in obvious ways. Check out the doors
    of your perception, asshole. Look around. Your dog is dead.

SCHEMATIC

Inside the machine is another machine, which refers to the machine enclosing it. So he touches her hand, and the image of a child emerges.

🦅

The steel ratchet in the wind: she felt it against her corneas, pressing precisely into the metric eye sockets, turning, tightening.

🦅

The elevator kept trembling: the mechanism out of key, but the riders held their eyes fixed on the dial, the reassuring arbitrary numbers.

🦅

Under the hood, where gear meshes integer, in the hamster wheel of the heart, a singularity appears, an homunculus, a social security number.

🦅

Wreckage washed ashore, fragments of fuselage and cowling, seat-backs, oxygen masks, and hermit crabs remade themselves of metal and bone.

🦅

A rat in the dark attic at midnight, bolt-cutter teeth incising insulation. Black wire, red wire. A spark. The pianist's hands stop playing.

🦅

The train enters the tunnel, great piston breaches the oily cylinder, clockwork tide is driven to foam on the rocks, and the marriage is over.

CASE HISTORY

We live in God's imagination,
    he whispers on the street to strangers.
He needs to take his medication,

But the angel of his unborn prescription
    squats with a sword of flame at the pharmacy door.
We live in God's imagination.

He sleeps in the black hole of a subway station,
    unexamined, unanalyzed, not able to remember
He needs to take his medication

So the voices of his inner congregation
    will sing in tune again. If he could be sure
We live in God's imagination,

Seamlessly as neurons in a ganglion,
    he might stop twitching. And how much more
He needs to take his medication

Depends on the contrail that tortures the event horizon
    incising above the square its insidious either/or.
We live in God's imagination.
    He needs to take His medication.

NOTES FOR AN EPITAPH

Thank breath, fire, and earth
for the accident of birth
Thank earth, fire, and breath
for the certainty of death

II

EITHER/OR

EITHER

What does the phrase "on the one hand" mean
    to the pregnant Iraqi seamstress
When the bomb goes off? Years later
    she will have learned to handle the needle
Miraculously, using her sculpted stump
    to smooth the fabric as her daughter,
Deaf by prenatal accident, shadows her, learning.

/

There is a boundary in the dark, the children know,
    which no one crosses. Its existence is a truth
Supported by every song and story. Nights
    after television, they stand at the open window
Staring beyond the swing set, the innocent hedgerow,
    and the bone-strewn no-man's-land, to the forest,
Where parents prepare their poisonous potions and stoke
    the ovens' fires, hungry but still afraid to go deeper
To the sulfurous caves the grandparents dug with iron blades
    and tried to vanish into—grim holes, yes, but still
Better than going farther, to the place where, when
    a tree falls, metaphysics begins to matter.

OR

On the other hand, there is sunlight, an April noon,
    green-tiled roofs luminous but never blinding,
Heavy cars invisible in garages camouflaged
    by disciplined hedges—even the wisteria and climbing
Rose obedient to a glacial offstage will. And when the dead
    arrive, admiring, hospital gowns ectoplasmic
In static light, the sick girl in the upstairs bedroom
    laughs, so foreign do they look, clustered
Next to the brass mailbox, lifting their cameras, focusing.

III

EPHEMERA

EPHEMERA

The old woman sat naked in a wicker chair under a jacaranda tree at midnight, sprinkled with purple petals, dreaming of a handful of dust.

Everything in the house had to be put in boxes, even the tiniest object— because that is all death means—handled, wrapped, listed, stored.

It was gathering food among rocks in the arroyo, grasshopper mouse, no bigger than a thumb—then shadow, wings, owl, a silent puff of fur.

After the performance, she removed the sweat-stained costume and her makeup; then, because of the mirror, her face, which was now complete.

Days later, Monday, work, it was already forgotten, that moment in the dark when by synchronicity they climaxed together and were destroyed.

Hot wind, sand blown against plate glass, centuries now, and a fine-etched image emerges, a city, maybe, if anyone were there to see.

That metaphor is dead that says he plows a field and under the sweat of his plowing something writes itself in compost: dead metaphor it says.

Carrying grocery bags, he walks as far as he can through the scorched land without stopping to eat, or think, or pull out his rusted pistol.

*

They had wandered years though wilderness, looking, not noticing until the land cooled and greened around them that the children were gone.

*

I told you, he said to the gravestone, *someone will always be here, someone will remember the story*—as they lowered him, he said, *I told you.*

THEORY

The form is that of an anti-nature. It partakes
  of the turbulence of arc-light, the prismatic
Skyline of reconstructed cities. The form is non-
  repeating, a finite but monotonous series
Of lusterless prime numbers equal to the square
  root of entropy. It is impersonal but destructive,
A hook pattern clearly defined in the radar of its own pages.
  Sirens go off in the provinces, but the center
Of the capitol is peaceful, maintaining the quotidian—
  croissants on a translucent plate, espresso, the stock
Exchange. The form is expansive but non-totalizing.
  It will not admit essences or transcendence.
It has no state, but is inclusive of gases, rage, plutocracy.
  It is supercooled and volatile. In the shadow of a broken
Column, lovers lean into one another. They have already
  Entered the second circle. By twilight, no one
Will remember the other life, its fragile music, its perfume.

CANON

A man wakes terrified from a dream; he takes down a book of poems and reads, "A man wakes terrified from a dream . . ."

❧

On a shelf above the Ark, where a cherub, deploying tamed cyclones, supervised the dusting, God set his beloved collection of shrunken heads.

❧

What he had constructed contained all the necessary elements for levitation, but his ascension was thwarted by an opaque cloud of words.

❧

He might have slept, but the thump of blades on wood startled him, and the muffled screams ahead, and the fighting not to lose his place in line.

❧

She was reading a book on the bus: soldiers, betrayals, executions; it absorbed her as the bullet smashed the window just before her stop.

❧

All she found was vital, anything en masse a collection. After years, from the weight of the massed material (string, paper, dust), the house mutated.

❧

They wrote a wall in the forest; ages they raised it, letter by letter, and in the end they stood behind it, but the enemy was illiterate.

❧

The slaves brought stones from a quarry; they were made to shape them, pile them up, and ascend, blindfold, the stairway of their own sweat.

Moonlight through the harp cast a shadow of the angel gathering poems from the desktop, sucking their souls through to Poetry.

A terrified man sleeps, and in his dream he sees the body politic wake, terrified, remembering the poem that begins "A terrified man sleeps . . ."

INVENTORY

Hogsheads from the provinces. Bundles from caravans.
    Crude crates from the holds of ships. Urns of oil and wine.
Embroidered sacks of opium tied shut with silk twine.
    Thirty slaves. Women: eight. Men: nine. Sundry children.
And on the farthest dock, a pile of junk: cracked cudgels, broken
    bandoliers, body armor stained, punctured, and stove in,
Bloodied bits of uniform, cartons of buttons, dice, bone
    gathered from all quadrants of the Baghdad war zone,
Assorted boots, mismatched teeth, torturers' pliers, prisoners' confessions—
    all stamped with the governor's seal and symbol: *sort, record, burn.*

EVERYTHING THAT IS THE CASE

He was tired, and there was work to do, a desk-load
    of files, a telephone. Deadlines. And yet his mind
Refused. He could think of cut dahlias and the cheap
    vase on the laminated table. Never profit margins.
Instead an old china plate, blue willow, and the single sausage
    with its precious patina of grease—while just beyond
The horizon of consciousness hovered a forgotten image
    not from a dream, but the hypnogogic crucifixion
Of last night's insomnia: the earth as a blackening smudge pot
    tracing across the firmament its dark-matter
Spoor, viscous residues of everything dying, smog
    of extinguished virus, char of bromeliad and whale. . . .
But first the crazed plate. The files. A scattering
    of petals. And always the excellent sausage.

EVENING REPORT

From a rural hilltop we observed unusual lights
    just above the horizon: diffused illumination
Like sheet lightning, though of greater intensity,
    and while it is true that after some minutes
A low rumbling reached us, we agreed it was not thunder,
    its pitch and periodicity being too unpredictable.
One of us remembered how, in the ancient songs,
    angels appeared to shepherds, and our sheep
Were, in fact, unsettled by the sky, and so we wondered.
    But by morning the shrapneled bodies were arriving, carted
Miles from the destruction, to be sorted and burned.
    Their anonymous smoke was observed by some
As a language of crosses over the vapor trails
    resurrecting themselves steadily on the eastern horizon.

MEMOIR

When they threw me into the pit, a shard of flint split
    my chin. I flicked it out of my jawbone and lay
In my leaking heap, regarding the fineness of its flesh-
    incising point. Up the black chimney of my prison
Vulture stars were circling, repeating all the familiar
    horrifying patterns. There was blood in the schist,
Of course, and a dried palm leaf. Before I died I learned
    to draw: scrap of meat, empty belly (that pictogram
An inspiration), club. And when the idiot children fell
    into my darkness and found what I'd done, it taught them
To sing my life while they kicked the weak one, growling curses
    and clawing each other blind for a turn beating rhythm
On the dusty fault lines of somebody's skull with a broken femur.

REPORT ON THE WESTERN TERRAIN

Acres of sandstone and aloe on this side of the river,
    starkest at sunset when even the lowest relief,
Even a soldier's body, overthrows its shadow.
    Then, after dusk, in moon-compounded twilight,
A peculiar abstraction appears, so that the mounds
    of corpses beyond the trenchwork grow
Colorless, their dissolving form so alien
    that even a casual observer would agree
This area is uncertain. And at midnight, a trained eye
    would be useless in the skirmish to contain
The language that reminds us how the other side
    of the stream supports a ratty cover of brambles,
Where another hidden scout writes out a ragged document
    in treacherous Braille, his report on the eastern terrain.

A CATALOG OF LANDSCAPES VIEWED
IN A CLAUDE GLASS

How moonlight breaks against planes of granite is a question,
    but moonlight breaks against boulders, moonlight is broken.
The black mirror makes plain the sublimity of its shards
    and bears over other scenes: the space where the blasted oak
Leans out of the dreary wind-beaten cliff, the space where the spring
    seeps through a ruptured wall beside an abandoned factory.
Hundreds of years ago the painter stood on a hillside overlooking
    a ruined little seaport in the south of France—a conundrum
Of dry rot and mildew, where even the rats had nothing
    but composted rope and trashed manifestos to eat—
And began to destroy more than nature ever intended
    with his incendiary strokes. And now we hold
The mirror as if it would shield us, as if the acidic light
    the painter deployed like napalm could be turned away
From the bodies visible to us nowhere but in this defining glass—
    mined soldiers, shopkeepers, a child still clutching a perfect ball.

FROM ABROAD

Every night in her childhood, going to sleep, she traveled
    the paths of the dead. It was easy then to go
Where she could not abide in her other consciousness.
    This was the avenue Caesar the mastiff had wandered.
Father said he had run away, and the children nodded solemnly
    knowing the kind old beast could hardly walk down the stairs.
And she could see there traces of Grandmother's passage—
    a bitch of a cruel cook who left smudges of pastry flour
Everywhere she touched. Along the inward-slanting road
    patches of it glowed with the faint luminescence
Of fungal rot. Night after night she assayed that way,
    going deeper with every journey. When Brother went under,
She thought: *now he will finally see me, now he will guide me*
    all the way in. But as she came to the battered gate
Beyond which he waited, she woke in the joy of her own sweat.
    Now all this returns to her. For years she had forgotten,
Believing the vaporous sleep of those who live their lives.
    What prose would it take, what pose, what ink and paper,
What postage, to send this note of reminder to the others
    still hanging back on the decent side of the ambivalent lintel?

GENOCIDES

It was like a hanging: being marched along streets with others, through great institutional doors, up stairs, to a desk, the groaning inbox.

※

They threw the bodies down the stairs, opened the warehouse door, rolled them inside, where the dead were logging hours on the loading dock.

※

Under the bridge, the alchemy of dawn is failing in its ancient transmutation, carbon dioxide and mercury sloughing off molecules of shit.

※

The final radiance arrives: everyone ossifies, tipping statues undercut by erosion, skeletons in derelict museums punching out, departing.

※

The lovers dressed, pulling underwear from under the chaise, stockings from the mantle, fur from bushes, hiding their feelers, hooves, horns.

※

Before they burned the bodies, they killed them; before they killed them they tortured them; before they tortured them, they gave them jobs.

※

Impossible not to forget the beautiful men, the children clever at their books, women full of wisdom, dead, my own body vaporized, my nation.

※

We were carrying bags from the grocer, polishing hammers, playing cards, dreaming of lost bodies, when the effacing brilliance distracted us.

Once we imploded the world enlarged, eroding every trace that anything had vanished, rain reclaiming our very atoms the better not to mourn us.

WORK ORDER

For the love of God, Montressor!
—POE

Stone is required. Mud. Wood. Strong hemp rope.
  A thousand barbarian slaves from the western provinces—
Dispensable, so let there be replacements ready on demand.
  The blueprints are completed, but the plan is simple: build it
Straight as a ray. Let no impure medium refract it.
  Make it as long as necessary. Make it even longer.
Make it too high for climbing, too adamantine for piercing,
  too deeply foundationed for radical undermining.
Make it as permanent as hatred. It is built to divide us
  from the others. Sweat is required. Blood. Crushed bone. Skin.
A river of bile and vitreous humor. Make it costly and perfect.
  When it is finished, the others will be cancelled.
It obliterates their eyes, their hair, the obscene color of their skin.
  When it is finished, a fatal peace will comfort
The survivors. When it is finished, and only then, let there be light.

REGISTRY OF THE CORPSES, THE ARRANGEMENT OF WHICH IS A REVERSE CHRONOLOGY ACCORDING TO DEATH DATE

—IRAQ, 2008

After the ship foundered, the hero, spared, entered the impossible mouth
    of the Underworld, and there encountered the bewildered
Soul of his third mate, just drowned on the stony beach where ribs
    and rigging, oars and wineskins, were scattered side by side
With the bodies. Dripping with ectoplasmic brine, the translucent one
    struggled to speak, his larynx ripped away by the cluster bombs
Of dying. There was a great mission, a quest, an indispensable question,
    but the hero was struck down by sorrow—the bowl of goat's blood
The gods had enjoined him to carry fell from his hands, and he turned
    back to forbidden daylight, where the bodies of his men,
Gull-pecked and slug-ridden now, he committed to flames and to decorous prayers.
    Only then did he go down again, now with a notebook and ballpoint pen,
Where the dead were properly arranged in an infinite row, waiting for him.
    Let the gods do their own dirty work. This was a human duty.
From the third mate back to the monkey, the spider, the amoeba,
    he gave them their proper place. He wrote them down.

EROTIC MANUAL

There are secrets unrealized by all but a few initiates,
    facts that transcend stimulation or the novelty of position.
Watch the way a seagull cracks open a clamshell by dropping it
    from a precisely calculated height onto a flat rock—
Too high and there's nothing worth lighting for, just bits of shell
    and a slick spot. The rock itself should be of adequate density
And large enough to target, but inconspicuous to competing predators.
    And the clam, *mysterium tremendum,* how to find
The indispensable, the fated, the inevitable, singular one
    without which the whole business is a travesty, a seedy melodrama,
Pointless, depressing violence: just one more meal?

A DESCRIPTION OF THE MECHANISM

Everything that is absent gathers. Warehouse doors
    stained the metallic color of smoke close
On their cargo of sleet. The toothed wheel moves
    its shadow closer. The old man feels
Its torque behind his forehead, ratcheting down.
    You should not speak about the dead, he writes. *About that*
Of which we know nothing, it is indecent even to think.
    I watch the belts and greasy gears
Of starlight meshing in the distance. I am silent,
    respecting his wishes. But the grit
In my finger joints troubles my long oblivion
    with its mindless grinding, painless here
Where pain cannot be thought, but mechanical
    and interminable, eroding, corrosive
As the acid wash that cleanses the killing floor.

PRACTICE MUSIC

What is less often mentioned is the exotic flavor of the hemlock
    meticulously prepared by a slave who distilled his craft
Decades from the whip and the alembic, courtesy of Phoenicia.
    This was not about ethics or honor. The old gourmand craved it.
Fatal, of course, but worth the months of stoic waiting
    in the Spartan cell, pacing, noodling on a harp.
Then the wooden cup. The fabulous nose. The complex
    flavor of taste buds dying. Applause. The click of a door unlocking.

MANIFEST

Appears suddenly caviar. Appears suddenly tungsten.
    Appears suddenly coltan, black gold from the Congo.
Appears suddenly a crate of uncut diamonds caked
    in a carbonaceous dust. The miracle of unconcealment
Conceals itself in the obviousness of sweat.
    Appears the opium poppy. Appears uranium.
Appears a knife between the ribs. Appears a kidney
    shrink-wrapped and iced down. Appears a decade
Of quite life in a gated suburb. An old woman paints
    the face of a counterfeit Rolex with radium,
Her teeth glowing in the factory dark. Appear succubi.
    Appear seraphim. The columns in the ledger fill
And overflow. Let there be titanium, let there be butter fish,
    let children block the doorway with their bags and masks.
Ex nihilo silver. *Ex nihilo* cattle. *Ex nihilo* pure cocaine.
    In the hold of the ship, in the railway car, the music of steel drums.

OBSERVATORY

Clear night sky scribbled to the margin with stars—that's the problem:
everything is written, no room even for a black hole. And God reads.

❧

A bountiful harvest season, everything ripening at the decisive moment,
whole galaxies tipped like so many apples beyond the event horizon.

❧

We lifted the brass tube: moons came into being, planetary rings, such
distances that our bodies faded to shadows in the obliterating lens.

❧

Tiny figure against the expanse of firmament, seen through the magnifying
gaze of something godlike with a crosshair and an ounce of lead.

❧

Safe in the great dome, at the end of the tube, she watched her lover at a
great distance enter the black hole, and the universe imploding.

❧

Two lenses moved randomly in her mind until they fell into the right
relation. She saw him clearly then, and cursed the perfection of focus.

❧

Light gathers in the perfect lens. Its restlessness is such that it cannot
remain there, even in perfection: it moves to clarify or destroy.

❧

Over great distance, the mechanism flattens what it reveals: dark matter, an
arc of stars, under an arch of oak limbs the lovers, made one.

INFINITE BY VIRTUE OF ITS
EVERLASTINGNESS

She was reading Keats by the fountain
    on an April morning. The iron bench
Was chilly, but the goldfish, excitable, rose
    readily to an offering of gnats.
And what was that urn singing? Christ!
    Only an hour left before the exam!
She started again, but the fountain
    was a distraction, the smear of forsythia
Beyond the copper fence, a car alarm
    blocks away. And what drew gnats to water—
A ticking insect thirst, or the light reflected there?
    Her boyfriend was handsome, but almost
Afraid to touch her. What was light to a gnat?
    What was water? No time. She wanted
To read, but her answer prevented her.
    What Keats was trying to say,
She wrote in her mind. *Trying to say.*

BOUNDED BY ITS OWN COMPLETENESS

Beyond the floodwall, flats: tide out or ocean
    evaporated, extinct—the photograph
Will be unforthcoming. But in the middle distance
    a gray smudge, bird-blur, establishes
That something has survived. He looks up
    from the viewfinder, satisfied.
Out of the parking lot behind him, synthesized
    Mozart, sound track of an ice cream truck,
And a single seagull rasp from the sky: the prophetic
    rat with wings has vaporized against the sun.

SINGULARITY

The work was done in her tiny garden, dark with the shadow of an office building that lay over her peonies like a bruise or an event horizon.

The labyrinth of gravity solved simply by converting string theory to thread, she slew the minotaur of density and floated out of history.

The grandmother told a story as they walked, of a girl walking with her grandmother into the forest, where a wolf and a girl told a story.

When the monkey she'd let in her bed revealed himself, she saw the problem with the Great Chain of Being was not the being, but the chain.

A nameless light in the night sky; the animal howls, gnaws his chain, and dies, not knowing the loss of the word "dog," the name "Pompeii."

We hymned to doctors; we chanted to priests; we ate strange powders, drank potions, fasted. When we died, our fever modulated into the key of sulfur.

The carnival of apocatastasis rolls into the galaxy not an eon too soon, setting up its canopy over the abyss so the sun can go out dancing.

The vortex on the pond where the water strider had been was the sign not of the something that took it but of the nothing that did not.

One moment in the steely galaxy a falcon gyred, then stalled in his striding on a ripple in the locus: then a spray of neutrinos: then void.

THE ILLEGIBILITY OF PROVIDENCE

The problem was opaque. She inserted two hooks—
    stainless steel, weighty, sterile—
Into his lower chest beneath the ribcage and drew him
    to her, extracting the whole structure of bone
Clean in that great attraction. He mistook
    what she wanted. There was a universe imploding,
and he thought the pain was his. A meteor shower,
    a comet, an eclipse: nothing foretold this.
Or perhaps he had simply failed to understand it.
    Another mistake I made, he thought, collapsing
On the overpriced carpet, finally and miraculously spineless.

ALGORITHMS FOR CALIBRATING PRECISE DISTORTION

A box of coins: one my fate, one my face, the others counterfeit. I close my eyes, reach in, choose: wrong, yes, but so it had been written.

The man with a headache reached into his mind and extracted a bit of shrapnel, which, examined, was the clone of a passage from Bach.

Signing the lien, he felt a twinge in his abdomen, as if someone were writing his own name on his belly with a pen of white phosphorus.

No one believed in demons, which made the exorcism a great success: there was dance, drink, and the guest of honor bleeding from the mouth.

Entropy broke through the café window, tipping a dish of cornichon, blinding the waiter with its radiation, emptying the diners' wallets.

Walking the shining hallway to the toilet, the busboy tripped over a marble head with a disgusted face, a patron who refused to leave a tip.

The slum in the heart of the flower, alley in the slum, door in the alley: in a grimy room, the homunculus sits, crippled, selling a flower.

As he went under anesthesia, the stockbroker dreamed the money he'd embezzled had written itself into a poem, and the poem into an epitaph.

THE UNWRITTEN HISTORY OF PROSE

> . . . a litel thyng. . . .
> —CHAUCER

The prose of merchants, the prose of ministers,
    pornographers' prose, the prose of Julius Caesar—
Every militant word. Executioners' prose, inspectors' prose,
    the dreamy calculation of love letters,
Attorneys' prose, morticians' prose,
    the coded prose of spies. One ice storm,
Years back, scribbled its thesis on Ohio.
    In another, my father, still alive, incised my name
Backward in rime on the kitchen window.
    He stood outside in the world, ice in his eyebrows,
Breathing. My neighbor has no dog run.
    My father built one for his brace of English pointers
Who howled their misery in doggy paragraphs
    as the storm revised them. I was old enough to read
Three words, and he'd just scraped one of them
    in front of his blood-lit face.
                      The prose of sociologists,
Alchemists' Latin prose, the cookbook prose of chefs,
    memory's watery pages—how to map its geology, its chalky strata,
Volcanic upheavals, sediments of excrement and ash?
    Someone lies in a bedroom illuminated by ice-light
As the storm cracks down. On the hearth, a small fire;
    on the table, a sheaf of parchment; by the door,
Twitching in sleep, an indeterminate dog.
    The man composes in his head. *I wol yow telle*
A litel thyng in prose, he might be thinking.

ABANDONED DRAFT

Light slants, and a character enters, a stranger here, but the horizon is
untroubled by the intrusion, and the cattle are undisturbed, and the
lakeshore—nothing here notices the solitary figure with obscure qualities
who walks out of concealment into the field of vision, just as nothing in
the field of vision hinders this passage. The body goes on. Ignorance is
required to go on, ignorance of something, if not of a god then of oneself,
or one's anti-self, of language, or of ignorance itself—something like that
is necessary, foot by foot, sentence by sentence, catachresis by iamb,
something unspeakable is necessary to go on

RERUNS OF THE APOCALYPSE

It was theirs. They stood by the water at dusk, lovers scarred by the violence of their alchemy, transmuting the darkness at the skyline.

🐦

It was not theirs. The boundaries betrayed them. Out of the core of their argument a shape arose, arsenical whirlwind, last word.

🐦

It was no one's. A destroying wave passed through Being, positron to pulsar, invisible, unknown to them as they removed each other's skin.

🐦

It was human. A double knot in the double helix hardwired them not to fate but inevitable accident: one molecule awry, everything collapses.

🐦

It was not human. The bridges into the city were empty at midnight, the trains were silenced, bars dark: one great godflash, and lights out.

🐦

It was natural. Rivers divorced seas under the aegis of ending, tectonic plates shattered against apartment walls, all evolving closure.

🐦

It was never natural, not cosmic rays unspooling, epic failure of photosynthesis. The lovers were fuse and timer, thrusting seconds home.

🐦

One last morning under the pergola we discussed what had happened in the godhead's crucible, but the fruit distracted us, we lost the thread, you touched my hand, and we were smoke.